TROUT

GW00657513

220
Favourite
Flies

For Trout, Salmon,
Sea-trout & Grayling

emap

Edited by
Sandy Leventon, John Wilshaw,
Andrea Longhurst and Julian Cooke

ISBN 0 9533087 2 3

Printed in Poland

Produced by
Publishing Promotions
1 High Street
Princes Risborough
Bucks HP27 0AG

Published by
Emap Active Ltd
Bushfield House
Orton Centre
Peterborough PE2 5UW

Contents

Flies
for all
seasons

Compiling a book about favourite flies is a fascinating job: which flies should we include? Which ones should we decide to omit?

During our time on *Trout and Salmon* magazine literally thousands of patterns have passed through our hands. All have caught fish, but some have proved deadlier than others. You can be assured, therefore, that all the flies featured in this book are tried and tested patterns. There are no dubious nine-day wonders here, created by fishermen more anxious to get their names in the history books than to help their fellow fishers.

Still in tune with the times
In these modern, hi-tech times it is rather nice to be able to feature flies that were regarded as household names in our grandfathers' day: old-fashioned they may be; obsolete they most certainly aren't!

Right, flies aplenty on this fisher's waistcoat.

For ease of reference we have divided the book into sections. Where we think it appropriate we have also suggested hook sizes. In the case of imitative trout flies these are precise, but so far as the sea-trout and salmon flies are concerned, they are for guidance only, water temperature, height and whether the fly is to be fished on a floating or sinking line all having an influence.

Tie your own or made to measure?

Whether or not you tie your own flies, we do hope that you will find this book useful. If you do 'roll your own' we give the recipe for making each fly. If you do not, merely give the tying details to

A cap makes a fine storage area for the day's selection – but do make sure the hooks don't go rusty.

one of the many excellent commercial fly-tyers who advertise in *Trout and Salmon* and they will be happy to fulfil your order.

We believe that the flies featured in these pages will serve you well wherever you fish. Their inclusion has been based on the fact that they are all proven fish-catchers.

Sandy Leventon
Editor,
Trout and Salmon

Salmon
flies

Why does a non-feeding salmon take an artificial fly? No one truly knows, but the patterns in this section have worked their magic on waters worldwide.

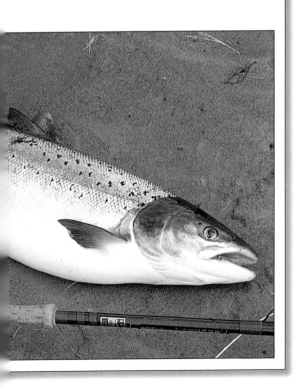

Claret Shrimp

Of all the shrimpy patterns, this one is regarded by many Irish, and a growing number of Scottish salmon-fishers, as the pick of the crop. It can be fished with confidence on rivers big and small, and in a wide variety of conditions.

Hook: *Size 8-12*
Thread: *Black*
Tag: *Golden-pheasant breast feather*
Rear body: *Claret seal's fur*
Middle hackle: *Rich claret*
Front body: *Dark claret seal's fur*
Rib: *Fine gold tinsel through both parts of the body*
Front hackle: *Two turns of hot-orange cock under two turns of badger*
Eyes: *Jungle cock*

Halpin

This bright fly is an excellent 'change' pattern when fishing an autumn river. Give it an extended trial when the water is clear and the day is blessed with the odd glimmer of sunshine.

Hook: *Size 6-8*
Thread: *Black*
Tag: *Fine oval tinsel*
Tail: *Golden-pheasant topping*
Butt: *Red wool*
Rib: *Oval silver tinsel*
Body: *Black floss silk*
Hackle: *Dyed red cock*
Throat: *Pale-blue dun*
Wing: *Grey squirrel with a golden-pheasant topping over*
Head: *Red varnish*

Beltra Badger

Anyone contemplating fishing for spring salmon on Lough Beltra should never go afloat without several of these flies in their box. It is usually positioned on the dropper.

Hook: *Size 4-10*
Thread: *Black*
Tag: *Fine round silver and yellow floss*
Tail: *Golden-pheasant topping*
Butt: *Black ostrich herl*
Body: *Flat silver tinsel*
Body hackle: *Lemon yellow from the second turn of the tinsel*
Rib: *Oval silver tinsel*
Wing: *Badger hair over a few fibres of red bucktail with a topping over all*
Throat: *Bright-blue cock*
Head: *Black*

Greg's Glory

A standard pattern on the Beauly, this
sharply dressed fly is making a name for
itself on rivers large and small in both
Scotland and Ireland.

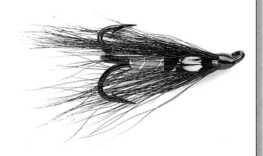

Hook: *Size 6-10. The smaller sizes are tied on
Partridge extra-longshank sea-trout trebles*
Thread: *Black*
Body: *In two parts – orange floss behind black floss*
Rib: *Oval silver*
Wing: *Black bucktail distributed
evenly around the shank*
Cheeks: *Jungle cock. A version for summer
fishing has a wing of squirrel hair with a couple of
pearly strands over*

Taylor Special

While it may look like the work of a
fly-dresser wearing a blindfold, this
gaudy little number is a fly that no angler
planning a trip to Ireland's River Moy should
be without.

Hook: *Size 6-12*
Thread: *Black*
Tag: *Oval silver tinsel*
Tail (optional): *Peacock sword fibres*
Body: *Front half, peacock herl; rear half,
fluorescent-green floss*
Rib: *Oval silver tinsel*
Veiling: *Single strand fluorescent-green
floss over rear half of the body*
Wing: *Grey squirrel tail dyed green*
Hackle: *Yellow cock*

Conway Blue

An old fly making something of a comeback on the rivers of North Wales for both sea-trout and salmon. A thinly tied version is regarded as excellent medicine when the water is low and clear.

Hook: *Size 6-8*
Thread: *Blue*
Tag: *Round silver thread and yellow floss*
Tail: *Golden-pheasant crest*
Butt: *Black ostrich herl*
Rib: *Oval silver tinsel*
Body: *Royal blue seal's fur*
Hackles: *Black and blue dyed cock*
Front hackle: *Jay*
Wing: *Two golden-pheasant tippet feathers tied back-to-back roofed with bronze mallard fibres and topping over*

Morrum Fly

A spate stream losing its power and colour following a downpour is the ideal place to try this shrimpy-looking pattern. An established killer of both salmon and sea-trout on the Swedish river from which it takes its name.

Hook: *Size 4-10*
Butt: *Oval silver followed by red floss*
Body: *Black floss*
Rib: *Oval silver tinsel*
Body hackle: *Palmered red
golden-pheasant body feather*
Throat hackle: *Teal fibres*
Wing: *Golden-pheasant tippets with
golden-pheasant tail fibres over*

Stuart's Killer

Hailing from the River Spey, this old fly has a
reputation for doing great deeds with both
salmon and sea-trout. When seeking salmon,
the fly should be dressed quite thinly.

Hook: *Size 6-12*
Thread: *Black*
Tail: *Red dyed hackle fibres*
Body: *Flat silver*
Rib: *Oval gold tinsel*
Wing: *Golden-pheasant tippets overlaid
with bronze mallard fibres*
Cheeks: *Jungle cock*
Hackle: *Dyed red hen*

Orange-and-Gold Waddington

A great fly for coloured water or rivers carrying a peat stain. Fish it with a steady retrieve in the slower pools and glides. The lower the water, the sparser the dressing should be. Excels on a sunny day.

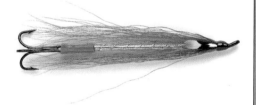

Hook: *1-3-inch Waddington shank*
Body: *Gold mylar or wide tinsel*
Rib: *Oval gold tinsel*
Wing: *Hot-orange bucktail*
Cheeks: *Jungle cock (optional)*

Gold Sylph

Give this bright little fly an extended trial
when grilse are lying in thin water on a day
of broken clouds and bright sunshine.

Hook: *Size 8-10*
Thread: *Black*
Tail: *Golden-pheasant topping*
Body: *Flat gold tinsel*
Rib: *Fine oval silver tinsel*
Wing: *Bronze mallard slips tied low
over the body*
Hackle: *Lemon hackle fibres followed
by a golden-pheasant yellow breast feather
drawn down to a beard*

Thunderflash

Inventor Robert Rattray designed the fly for
fishing on an autumn day with a floating line.

Hook: *Size 6-10*
Thread: *Black*
Body: *Butting turns of oval gold, varnished*
Hackle: *Hot-orange cock*
Underwing: *Four strands of gold Lureflash*
Wing: *Black squirrel*
Overwing: *Few strands of pearl Krystal Flash
extending past the black hair*

Sheila

A fly with a reputation for taking fresh fish. Carry versions with varying amounts of orange hackle – the thinner the water, the less hackle the fly should have.

Hook: *Size 6-12*
Thread: *Black*
Tail: *Golden-pheasant crest*
Body: *Flat gold tinsel*
Rib: *Fine silver tinsel or copper wire*
Hackle: *Orange cock*
Wing: *Black squirrel*

Fast Eddie

A modern pattern that has a growing reputation on the Thurso, especially in spring. The black-bodied version is said to be more readily accepted by resident fish.

Hook: *Size 4-10*
Thread: *Red*
Tag: *Three turns oval gold tinsel*
Body: *Flat gold mylar, or black floss*
Rib: *Oval gold*
Wing: *Green hair over yellow bucktail in larger sizes, squirrel for the smaller patterns*
Hackle: *Hot-orange hen.*
The Waddington version has a red tying thread tag, flat mylar body ribbed with broad oval gold; the wing is first yellow bucktail then orange, then green, with a few strands of yellow and pearl Crystal Hair next to the body. The head is red tying thread bisected with black

Emerald Stoat

This pattern has a reputation for taking
fish lying in a shrunken stream when other,
more conventionally bodied, flies have
been ignored.

Hook: Size 6-12
Thread: Black
Tag: Fine oval silver
Tail: Yellow cock hackle fibres with a few
strands of lime Crystal Hair
Body: Green lurex (or pearl mylar
over black tying thread)
Rib: Oval silver followed by fluorescent-green
floss (Glo-Brite No 12)
Wing: Black squirrel
Hackle: Black cock

Orange Lodge

Offer this bright fly to salmon that have settled following a spate and which have refused to be moved by more sombrely dressed patterns.

Hook: Size 6-12
Thread: Black
Body: Black floss
Rib: Broad flat silver tinsel
Wing: Hot-orange squirrel or bucktail
Hackle: Bright-blue cock

Munro Killer Longtail

Adding a mobile tail to a salmon fly has enhanced the performance of many successful salmon flies. By matching the size of the fly to the height and colour of the water, this updated fly can be used throughout the season with confidence.

Hook: *Size 10-14 longshank treble*
Thread: *Black*
Tail: *Black, yellow and red bucktail or similar, and a few strands of pearl Crystal Hair*
Body: *Black floss*
Rib: *Oval gold*
Wing: *Short black calf*
Throat hackle: *Orange cock with blue gallena over*
Cheeks: *Jungle cock*

Claret Tail Bann Special Shrimp

Anyone preparing for an Irish holiday should be sure to have this one in their boxes. It is particularly good when the water has dropped and the fish are confined to large, slow pools. Then, the winning tactic is to cast up and across what current there is, and to retrieve the fly slowly in a curve.

Hook: *Size 6-12*
Thread: *Black*
Tag: *Fine oval or flat silver*
Tail: *Golden-pheasant red breast feather dyed claret*
Body: *Rear-half, yellow floss; front-half, black floss*
Rib: *Fine oval silver*
Centre hackle: *Hot-orange*
Wings: *Jungle cock set as a 'roof'*
Head hackle: *Badger*
Head: *Black*

Grey-Winged Salmon Gosling

Never go afloat on an Irish lough in search of grilse without this fly in the box. Fish it with confidence in either dull or bright conditions.

Hook: *Size 8-10*
Thread: *Black*
Tail: *Cock pheasant tail fibres*
Body: *Golden-olive seal's fur*
Wing: *Grey mallard flank feather, doubled and wound as a hackle*
Hackle: *Hot-orange cock*

Silver Erriff

A super fly for grilse that excels when the
river is flowing clear. The lower the stream,
the smaller the fly should be.

Hook: *Size 6-10*
Tag: *Flat silver tinsel*
Tail: *Golden-pheasant topping*
Butt: *Black ostrich*
Rib: *Oval silver*
Body: *Flat silver*
Wing: *Badger hair over golden-pheasant topping over*
Hackle: *Kingfisher blue cock*

Brown Turkey

This spate-river special enjoys a reputation for taking fish in a summer flood, but which has yet to become stained with peat.

Hook: *Size 6-10*
Thread: *Black*
Tail: *Golden-pheasant tippets*
Body: *From the tail, dubbed blue, red and yellow seal's fur*
Rib: *Flat silver tinsel*
Wing: *Cinnamon turkey, brown hen or goose. The perfect feather has a whitish tip*
Hackle: *Blue jay fibres*

Cuileg

A firm favourite on the Beauly, this bright fly is at its best when grilse are lying in fast, clear water. Another version has yellow squirrel tail fibres at tail and throat. Both flies are more effective when lightly dressed.

Hook: *Size 6-10 double*
Thread: *Black*
Tail: *Orange squirrel tail*
Tag: *Fine oval gold*
Body: *Black floss*
Rib: *Two – fine oval gold over hot-orange floss*
Hackle: *Orange squirrel fibres*
Wing: *Black squirrel to reach to the tip of the tail*

Juner Shrimp

A native of the Moy fishery, this fly takes its name from the time when the grilse start to run that prolific Irish fishery in earnest. It is a noted taker of fish when the water is cold, or when the wind is blowing from the north.

Hook: *Size 6-12 treble, double or single*
Thread: *Black*
Tag: *Oval gold tinsel*
Tail: *Golden-pheasant red breast feather*
Body: *Rear-half, red seal's fur or floss; front-half, purple seal's fur or floss*
Centre hackle: *Yellow*
Rib: *Fine gold tinsel*
Front hackle: *Purple*
Head: *Black*

Stinchar Stoat's Tail

A great killer of salmon and sea-trout that is particularly effective when the water is low and clear. A useful rule of thumb is to reduce the size of hook and the amount of dressing as the water falls.

Hook: *Size 4-10*
Thread: *Black*
Tag: *Four turns of oval silver tinsel*
Tail: *Golden-pheasant topping*
Body: *Black floss*
Rib: *Medium oval silver tinsel*
Wing: *Black squirrel*
Hackle: *Hot-orange tied as a collar*
Cheeks: *Jungle cock (optional)*
Head: *Black*

Irish General Practitioner

Many anglers consider this version to be more effective than the original pattern when fishing in coloured water or over fresh fish. Variants dressed with bodies of fiery brown, claret or golden-olive are preferred for resident fish in clearer water.

Hook: *Size 8-12*
Thread: *Black*
Tag: *Flat or oval gold*
Tail: *Golden-pheasant red breast feather with a short V-shaped tippet feather as a top veiling*
Rear body: *Orange seal's fur*
Rear hackle: *Palmered hot orange*
Rib: *Medium or fine oval gold tinsel*
Veiling: *A short tippet feather or strands on top only*
Front body: *Hot-orange seal's fur*
Front hackle: *Palmered hot-orange hackle*
Rib: *Fine oval gold tinsel*
Veiling: *Golden-pheasant red breast feather laid on top*
Head: *Red or black*

Apache Shrimp

A shrimp-style fly with a difference and the
one to tie on when less colourful patterns
fail. The long mobile tail makes it an ideal fly
for fishing in slackish water. Retrieve
in four- to nine-inch pulls.

Hook: *Size 6-12*
Thread: *Black*
Tag: *Flat or oval silver*
Rear hackle: *Golden-pheasant red breast feather*
Rear body: *Yellow floss*
Rib: *Oval silver*
Centre hackle: *Yellow or cock hen*
Front body: *Scarlet floss*
Rib: *Oval silver*
Front hackle: *Soft red cock*
Head: *Black varnish*

Briggs' Pennell

Never be without this fly when you fish a
spate river, especially when a breeze kicks
up a ripple on the slower pools. Fish it on
either a floating or sinking line.

Hook: *Size 8-12*
Thread: *Black*
Rib: *Flat silver tinsel*
Tail: *Golden-pheasant tippets*
Body: *Black seal's fur*
Hackle: *Natural black hen*

Glowing Ember

This jack-of-all-trades can be used throughout the season. The proportions of each colour can be altered to suit the conditions, a rule of thumb being that a clearer water demands a darker fly.

Hook: *Size 4-10*
Tail: *Golden-pheasant topping*
Body: *Black floss*
Rib: *Oval silver tinsel*
Wing: *Below – squirrel tail, orange over yellow over red. Above – black squirrel*
Cheeks: *Jungle cock (optional)*
Head: *Black*

Orange-and-Gold Shrimp

Thought by many as one of the best
spate-river flies invented, this is a reliable
offering when fishing over both fresh or
resident fish the season through.

Hook: *Size 6-12*
Tag: *Flat, oval gold or silver tinsel*
Tail: *Golden-pheasant red breast feather*
Body: *Rear-half, oval gold tinsel; front-half,
black seal's fur*
Centre hackle: *Hot-orange cock*
Rib: *Oval gold tinsel*
Front hackle: *Badger*
Head: *Black*

Ghost Shrimp

Combine a bright summer day, fish running in a falling flood, and you have the perfect opportunity to tie on this sharply dressed killer of grilse.

Hook: *Size 6-12*
Thread: *Black*
Tag: *Oval or flat silver*
Tail: *Golden-pheasant breast feather*
Rear body: *Yellow floss ribbed with oval silver*
Veilings: *Orange hackle points*
Centre hackle: *White*
Front body: *Black floss*
Rib: *Oval silver*
Veilings: *As rear body*
Wings: *Jungle cock*
Head hackle: *Badger cock*
Head: *Black*

Grey Squirrel

At its best on medium to small rivers running high and clear after a summer flood. A firm favourite with fishers on the River Annan. Dressed on small hooks, it is a reliable fly for sea-trout in the same conditions.

Hook: *Size 4-10*
Thread: *Black*
Tag: *Flat gold tinsel*
Tail: *Golden-pheasant topping*
Butt: *Black ostrich*
Body: *Black floss*
Rib: *Fine flat gold tinsel*
Wing: *Sparse grey squirrel*
Hackle: *Pale blue cock*

Goat

Regarded by many Irish salmon-fishers as a first-choice pattern for both fresh and resident fish, it probably gives of its best in peaty water and a sunny day.

Hook: *Size 6-10*
Thread: *Black*
Tag: *Oval silver*
Butt: *Black seal's fur*
Body: *Light-grey seal's fur*
Rib: *Oval silver tinsel*
Wing: *Yellow squirrel*
Hackle: *Yellow cock*

Green Highlander

While there are a few Highland rivers where green does well, this fly is better known on Scandinavian waters where traditional British patterns are still very popular.

Hook: *Size 4-10*
Thread: *Black*
Tag: *Silver tinsel*
Tail: *Golden-pheasant topping and wood duck*
Body: *Yellow floss then green floss, wool or dubbing*
Wing: *Brown hair over yellow over orange-dyed squirrel*
Hackle: *Green cock under yellow*
Cheeks: *Golden-pheasant red breast feather*

Hunter

Probably best known on the Tweed, this striking fly can be fished with confidence in the gloaming of a late-summer evening.

Hook: *Size 4-8*
Thread: *Black*
Body: *Rear half, red floss palmered with dark-red hackle; front half, black floss palmered with black hackle*
Rib: *Oval silver tinsel*
Wing: *Slips of white turkey, goose or swan*
Head hackle: *Blue jay (optional)*

Ian Wood

Any fly that took seven salmon weighing nearly 80 lb from Loch Lomond in a single day deserves an extended trial when fishing for both loch sea-trout and salmon. It is particularly effective when fished on the bob and was invented by the first editor of *Trout and Salmon*, who sometimes tied it without a hackle.

Hook: *Size 6-10*
Thread: *Black*
Tail: *Golden-pheasant topping*
Body: *Flat gold tinsel*
Rib: *Fine oval gold*
Wing: *White-tipped turkey feather*
Hackle: *Ginger cock*

Arndilly Fancy

This striking fly, invented on the Arndilly beat
of the Spey, takes fish far from its birthplace
and is particularly effective fished on a
floating or sink-tip line in late spring.

Hook: *Size 4-10*
Tag: *Oval silver*
Tail: *Topping*
Body: *Yellow floss*
Rib: *Oval silver*
Throat: *Bright-blue cock*
Wing: *Black squirrel*
Cheeks: *Jungle cock*
Head: *Two-thirds red; one-third black*

Ally's Shrimp

The fly that can be fished anywhere and at any time with total confidence from late spring to late autumn has yet to be devised, but Alastair Gowans's long-tailed creation comes pretty close.

Hook: Size 6-12
Thread: Red
Tail: Strands of long hot-orange bucktail
Body: Rear half, red floss; front half, black floss
Rib: Oval silver
Wing: A bunch of grey squirrel with golden-pheasant tippets over
Hackle: Grey squirrel tied as a beard
Collar: Long hot-orange cock
Head: Red

Assassin

Bearing a marked family resemblance to the
Silver Invicta, this pretty fly does well for
both salmon and sea-trout in clear water
before strong light touches the stream.

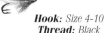

Hook: *Size 4-10*
Thread: *Black*
Tag: *Oval silver tinsel*
Tail: *Golden-pheasant topping*
Body: *Flat silver tinsel divided in the centre by a
yellow cock hackle*
Rib: *Oval silver*
Wing: *Natural red squirrel. Natural bucktail
tied short in the larger sizes*
Hackle: *Grouse or partridge under a few blue jay fibres*

Silk Cut Shrimp

This pattern originated from the Ally's Shrimp. Although purple is regarded as a summer/autumn colour, this fly is known for taking a great number of late-spring fish.

Hook: *Size 4-10*
Thread: *Black*
Tail: *Long purple bucktail with a sparse addition of Crystal Hair*
Body: *Flat pearl lurex over wet varnishing tying silk, with varnish over the completed body for protection*
Wing: *Golden-pheasant tippet feather dyed purple, tied to lie horizontal*
Collar: *Purple hen or cock, long and full*
Head: *Black*

Copper King

Clad in the hues of autumn, this simple hairwing is a great killer of fish as the season draws to its close. It is particularly effective on spate rivers carrying a touch of colour.

Hook: *Size 4-10*
Thread: *Black*
Body: *Copper tinsel*
Rib: *Copper wire*
Wing: *Equal mixture of red and yellow bucktail dressed all around the shank*

Executioner

A super fly for both salmon and sea-trout.
Fish it on a floating line in the thin streams
of summer.

Hook: *Size 6-12*
Silk: *Red*
Tag: *Fine oval silver*
Tail: *Yellow cock*
Body: *First quarter, Glo-Brite no. 4 fluorescent
floss; remainder, flat silver*
Rib: *Fine oval silver*
Hackle: *Black cock*
Wing: *Black squirrel*
Cheeks: *Jungle cock*
Head: *Red*

Black-and-Red Waddington

A good fly in clear, low water. An excellent
offering when salmon have settled into a lie.
Fish it with the flow or with long, slow pulls.

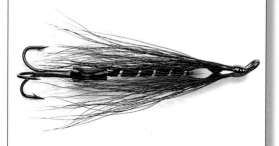

Hook: 1-3-inch Waddington shank
Body: Black floss
Rib: Oval gold or silver tinsel
Wing: Black bucktail with red underneath
Cheeks: Jungle cock (optional)

Stoat's Tail

Fished on a floating line, black flies produce an unmissable silhouette and the Stoat's Tail is perhaps the most famous of all these warm-water flies.

Hook: *Size 6-12*
Tag: *Oval silver tinsel*
Body: *Black floss*
Rib: *Silver tinsel*
Hackle: *Black cock*
Wing: *Stoat's tail hairs or black squirrel*

Black Dart

One to tie on with confidence when a spate
stream has cleared to the colour of strong
ale. It seems to give of its best when given a
thin wing and a portly body.

Hook: *Size 6-10 and tubes*
Thread: *Black*
Body: *Black floss over fine lead wire*
Rib: *Oval gold tinsel*
Wing: *Orange bucktail*
Cheeks: *Jungle cock*

Hairwing Black Doctor

This member of the practice is regarded as good medicine for a small-river summer salmon that has settled into a lie following a spate.

Hook: *Size 4-10*
Thread: *Black*
Tag: *Silver tinsel*
Tail: *Golden-pheasant topping*
Butt: *Bright-red wool*
Body: *Black floss*
Rib: *Fine oval silver*
Wing: *Blue, yellow and orange hair topped with a brown-dyed grey squirrel hair*
Hackle: *Blue dyed guineafowl*
Head: *Red varnish*

Black Maria

An excellent floating-line pattern, whose contrasting body colours and half-palmered hackle provide an attractive silhouette.

Hook: *Size 4-10*
Tag: *Oval silver*
Tail: *Golden-pheasant topping*
Body: *Rear half, yellow; front half, black floss*
Rib: *Oval silver*
Hackle and throat: *Black over the black floss*
Wing: *Black squirrel or bucktail*

Black-Green Highlander Templedog

Since its introduction to this country from
Sweden, this fly has taken fish all over
Scotland. It is particularly good on the Tweed
in autumn, where it should be fished,
unweighted, on a fast-sinking line.

Hook: *1-3-inch tube* **Tag:** *Oval gold tinsel*
Butt: *Fluorescent-green Antron* **Body:** *Underbody of
yellow floss* **Body:** *Rear two-thirds, flat gold embossed
tinsel; front third, black seal's fur or substitute* **Rib:** *Oval
gold tinsel* **Body hackle:** *One yellow and one Green
Highlander-shade cock hackles stripped on one side and
wound together* **Wing:** *In this order – strands of yellow-
dyed polar bear or other stiff hair as underwing,
fluorescent-yellow Krystal Flash, green Flashabou, yellow,
green hot-orange fox hair, dark-brown fox hair, bronze
peacock herl, Flashabou dubbing/Lite Brite in dark
green, chartreuse, yellow and orange combed into the fox
hair. The final layer is black fox hair covering two-thirds
of the wing* **Cheeks:** *Jungle cock* **Head:** *Black*

Hairy Mary

A very famous fly for all waters, particularly those of the Highlands and west coast of Scotland.

Hook: *Size 6-12, singles and doubles*
Thread: *Black*
Tag: *Fine oval gold*
Tail: *Golden-pheasant crest, or yellow hackle fibres (in big sizes)*
Body: *Black floss*
Rib: *Oval gold*
Throat: *Mid-blue cock*
Wing: *Barred brown squirrel or fine brown bucktail in large sizes*
Head: *Black*

Garry D

One of the first hairwing salmo[n] ... this country, it has spawned a nost of variants, Many of them are proven killers in a stream touched with colour, especially at the back end of the season.

Hook: *Single, double, treble, tubes and Waddingtons*
Thread: *Black*
Body: *Black floss or wool*
Rib: *Oval silver*
Wing: *Yellow bucktail over red*
Hackle: *Dyed-blue guineafowl*

Willie Gunn

Rivalled only by the Ally's Shrimp and the Stoat's Tail as the most popular salmon pattern, the Willie Gunn can be fished with confidence in almost every situation. Just change the size to suit the water conditions.

Hook: *Singles, doubles and trebles, tubes and Waddingtons*
Thread: *Black*
Body: *Black floss*
Rib: *Oval gold tinsel*
Wing: *Even mix of yellow, orange, red and black hair*
Head: *Black*

Usk Grub

One of the earliest salmon Shrimp patterns,
the Usk Grub has stood the test of time and
is still as deadly as ever.

Hook: *Size 6-10*
Tag: *Silver thread*
Rear hackle: *Golden-pheasant breast feather*
Body: *Rear half, dull orange (optionally veiled with
scarlet cock hackle tips)*
Centre hackles: *White and orange cock*
Body: *Front half, seal's fur*
Rib: *Silver thread*
Front hackle: *Paired jungle cock*

61

Munro Killer

This, the most famous of Spey flies, is best fished on a floating line. Its wing should be about 1½ times the length of the hookshank.

Hook: *Size 4-10*
Tag: *Oval gold*
Tail: *None*
Body: *Black silk*
Rib: *Gold*
Throat: *Mixture of orange strands and blue guineafowl*
Wing: *Black over yellow (or grey squirrel)*

Jerram's Fancy

Reminiscent of the Camasunary Killer, this unusually coloured fly does well in peaty water for both salmon and sea-trout.

Hook: *Size 6-12*
Thread: *Black*
Tag: *Oval silver tinsel*
Tail: *Bright-blue feather fibres*
Body: *Rear, red floss; front, black floss*
Rib: *Fine oval silver tinsel*
Wing: *Black squirrel*
Hackle: *Blue cock fibres tied as a beard*

John Anthony Shrimp

Homespun it may look, but this simple Shrimp caught countless salmon on Ireland's Owenea River for its inventor. It has the reputation of excelling in difficult conditions.

Hook: *Size 6-12*
Tag: *Oval gold*
Tail: *Golden-pheasant red breast feather*
Rear body: *Black floss or seal's fur*
Rib: *Oval gold tinsel*
Middle hackle: *Red game*
Front body: *Black floss or seal's fur*
Rib: *Fine oval gold*
Wings (optional): *Jungle cock*
Front hackle: *Red game*

Krabla

This shrimpy creation from Iceland could well
be the one to turn the tables on a salmon
that has seen everything in the book.

Hook: *Size 4-6*
Thread: *White*
Tail: *Soft white fur or marabou*
Antennae: *Two pink and two white stripped
hackle stalks*
Body: *Pink and white saddle hackles wound together
and trimmed to shape*

Editor

Devised by *Trout and Salmon* editor Sandy
Leventon, this fly positively gleams in the
water and is particularly effective for spring
salmon, whether fished on a floating,
intermediate or sinking line. The wing should
be 1½ times the length of the hookshank.

Hook: *Size 2-10*
Thread: *Black*
Underbody: *White Antron*
Body: *Pearl Lurex*
Rib: *Fluorescent-green nylon (18 lb for flies
size 2-6; 12 lb for smaller)*
Hackle: *Blue cock*
Wing: *Black bucktail*
Cheeks: *Jungle cock*

Yellow Dolly Muddler

A variation of Derek Knowles's original
Yellow Dolly, this Muddler version is a fly to
try when all else has failed. Its wake often
brings up a dour salmon.

Hook: ¼ in-¾ in plastic tube
Head: Spun deerhair
Skirt: Yellow bucktail, trimmed short

Jeannie

A reliable pattern for summer's low water.
Fished on a floating line, it is also a good
sea-trout fly.

Hook: *Size 6-10*
Silk: *Black*
Tail: *Golden-pheasant crest*
Body: *Rear half, yellow floss; front half, black floss*
Rib: *Oval silver*
Hackle: *Black cock*
Wing: *Bronze mallard*
Cheeks: *Jungle cock*

Logie

With the water warming in early summer, the light-coloured Logie will often bring up a fish when more popular patterns such as a Munro Killer have failed.

Hook: *Size 4-10*
Thread: *Black*
Tag: *Round gold tinsel*
Tail: *Golden-pheasant crest*
Body: *In two halves; rear half, yellow floss; front half, red floss*
Rib: *Oval silver tinsel*
Hackle: *Dyed-blue cock*
Wing: *Squirrel tail, yellow under brown*

Old Charlie

Looking for all the world like the mating between a Thunder and Lightning and a Hairy Mary, it can be used with confidence when fishing for grilse in low water and in autumn when the water is not too coloured.

Hook: *Size 4-8*
Thread: *Black*
Tag: *Flat gold tinsel*
Tail: *Golden-pheasant topping*
Body: *Dark claret floss*
Rib: *Oval gold tinsel in wide-spaced turns*
Wing: *Natural brown bucktail or black-barred red squirrel for the smaller sizes*
Hackle: *Hot orange tied as a beard*
Eyes: *Jungle cock (optional)*

Silver-Blue Micro Tube

One to try when the river has shrunk to its
bones and lethargic salmon have refused all
other offerings.

Body: *Half-inch plastic tube wide enough
to take a size 14 treble*
Wing: *Blue bucktail tied evenly around the tube,
and two strands of silver tinsel secured on one side
of the fly*

Sea-trout

The fickle sea-trout
must often be seduced
by special patterns.
Those that follow should
do the trick!

Blackie

Gives of its best offered hard on the bottom
in early season. One of the very best
sea-trout lures, it should be fished close
to the surface on a Bible-black night or
slowly down in the deeps when nothing
stirs the surface.

Hook: *Size 6, 8 and 10 and in tandem form*
Thread: *Black*
Tail: *Black hackle fibres*
Body: *Black seal's fur*
Rib: *Silver wire*
Hackle: *Long black cock*
Wing: *Black squirrel*
Cheeks: *Jungle cock. The tandem version has a long
wing reaching over both hooks*

Zulu

The Zulu has a worldwide reputation as a killer of sea-trout and is popular as a general lake pattern, fished from a boat as a top dropper.

Hook: *Size 8-14*
Tail: *Red wool or ibis*
Body: *Black wool or seal's fur with a palmered black cock hackle*
Rib: *Fine flat silver tinsel*
Head hackle (optional): *Black cock or hen*

Doon Fry

A fly that is readily accepted by sea-trout lying in very thin water, stillwater brown trout and rainbows feeding on fry. It has also accounted for some big estuary sea-trout.

Hook: *Size 8-10 double*
Thread: *White*
Tail: *White floss*
Body: *White floss ribbed with fine round silver tinsel*
Wing: *Bronze mallard*
Hackle: *Teal fibres*
Head: *Black*

Dovey Black and Orange

This is a 'must' fly when fishing for Welsh sea-trout in a wide range of river conditions. Fished on a floating line it can be lethal in the couple of hours before total darkness.

Hook: *Size 6-8 double*
Thread: *Black*
Body: *Black floss*
Rib: *Oval silver tinsel*
Wing: *Dyed-black squirrel*
Hackle: *Orange cock hackle fibres*
Eyes: *Jungle cock*

Baltic Special

Anyone with a fancy for fishing for sea-trout
in the estuaries should look no further than
this sparkling lure. Fish it quickly on an
intermediate line.

Hook: *Size 8 silvered longshank*
Thread: *Red*
Body: *Pearl Lureflash*
Wing: *Pearl Lureflash with blue Lureflash tied over*
Head: *Red*

Silver Ghost

A little fly capable of doing great things with
sea-trout just as the sun goes down. Fish it
in partnership with a version that has a flat
gold tinsel body.

Hook: *Size 10-14 doubles*
Thread: *Black*
Tail: *Golden-pheasant topping*
Body: *Flat silver tinsel*
Wing: *Natural grey squirrel tail*
Hackle: *Tied as a beard, blue jay in front of white*

Towy Topper

Fished on its own on a light leader, this is an excellent fly when taking on sea-trout hiding in the shadows of overhanging branches. Tied as a dry-fly, it is a first-rate pattern when they are lying in well-oxygenated water when the river is low.

Hook: *Size 8-12*
Thread: *Black*
Tail: *Golden-pheasant tippets*
Body: *Well-marked peacock quill*
Rib: *Fine silver wire*
Hackle: *Blue dun*

Black and Silver

Fish this one for night-time sea-trout,
especially when there's a glimmer of light
in the sky.

Hook: *1-1½-inch tube*
Body: *Flat silver tinsel*
Rib: *Oval silver tinsel*
Wing: *Black squirrel, goat or bucktail for
the larger sizes*

Blue Lightning Tube

This sandeel imitation is particularly effective
when fishing for big sea-trout newly arrived
from the sea.

Hook: *Two inches of ⅛-inch diameter plastic tube.
Widen one end to take the hook*
Body: *Medium purple mylar*
Wing: *Purple pearl Flashabou. Blue goat hair
overwing is optional*
Cheeks: *Jungle cock*
Head: *Red varnish*

Weasel

A first-rate pattern for sea-trout in a wide
range of water conditions, it is also an
excellent fly for salmon and grilse
in low water.

Hook: *Size 10-12 low-water doubles*
Thread: *Black*
Tag: *Four turns fine oval silver*
Tail: *Yellow cock hackle fibres*
Body: *Black floss ribbed with medium flat silver tinsel
in equal bands and then coated with clear nail varnish*
Wing: *Four fibres of Krystal Flash to reach the tip of
the tail, and a thin layer of black squirrel over*
Hackle: *Black cock*
Head: *Black with a central band of
fluorescent orange thread*

Silver Grey

This little Welsh sparkler comes into its own when the shoals of smaller sea-trout are fresh in from the tide. At its best in clear, fast water and on a day of broken cloud and sunshine.

Hook: *Size 8-12*
Thread: *Black*
Tail: *Golden-pheasant tippets*
Body: *Flat silver tinsel*
Rib: *Fine silver wire*
Wing: *Grey squirrel, tied short. The original used a well-marked teal flank feather*
Hackle: *Badger*

Red Twist

This sharply dressed fly is one of the best sea-trout flies designed in recent years. It is one of the few patterns that can be used with confidence during the day. An equally effective variant has a yellow butt and hackle. Both should be fished at range and on lightish leaders.

Hook: *Size 8-12 trebles*
Thread: *Black*
Butt: *Fluorescent-red floss*
Body: *Silver tinsel*
Rib: *Fine oval tinsel or wire*
Hackle: *Long-fibred red cock with black one over*

Purple Devil

Purple is a much underrated colour for both
salmon and sea-trout although there are
anglers who swear by any fly with purple in
its make-up. This one is a great favourite
with a few knowing Scottish sea-trout
fishers.

Hook: *Size 10-12*
Thread: *Black*
Tail: *Bunch of teal fibres*
Body: *Purple seal's fur*
Rib: *Fine oval gold tinsel*
Hackle: *Magenta cock*
Wings: *Bronze mallard*
Head: *Red*

Mallard and Orange

An old stager with a reputation for giving of
its best with autumn sea-trout, particularly
on the rivers Lune and Wenning.

Hook: *Size 8-12*
Thread: *Red*
Tag: *Gold wire*
Tail: *A bunch of orange cock hackles*
Body: *Orange seal's fur*
Hackle: *Orange*
Wings: *Bronze mallard*
Head: *Red*

Medicine Fly

This small fish imitation is a 'must' pattern for any sea-trout fisher, especially when the quarry is new from the sea.

Hook: *Size 4-10 low-water salmon irons*
Thread: *Red*
Body: *Silver tinsel*
Rib: *Oval silver tinsel*
Hackle: *Blue cock*
Wing: *Well-marked teal, mallard or wigeon*
Head: *Red*

Goat's Toe

Originally tied for the salmon and sea-trout
of the west of Ireland, it is a great catcher of
reservoir trout when fished on the dropper
on days of grey skies and rolling waves.

Hook: *Size 8-12*
Thread: *Black*
Tail: *Red wool or floss*
Body: *Bronze peacock herl*
Rib: *Red wool or floss*
Hackle: *Blue peacock neck feather*

Grey Monkey

Invented for the rivers of Ayrshire, this fly is
deadly at night, fished on a floating line.

Hook: *Size 8-12*
Thread: *Black*
Tail: *Barred teal feathers*
Body: *Rear half, golden-yellow floss or seal's fur;*
front half, grey monkey or grey seal's fur
ribbed with silver wire
Wing: *Wigeon*
Throat hackle: *Medium blue dun or grizzle*
Cheeks: *Jungle cock*

Huw Nain

A firm favourite with sea-trout anglers in
North Wales, this traditional fly enjoys the
remarkable reputation of having the power to
take sea-trout during the night and day.

Hook: *Size 6-8*
Thread: *Black*
Body: *Rear half, golden-olive seal's fur;
front half, grey seal's fur*
Rib: *Silver wire*
Wing: *Hen pheasant*
Hackle: *Partridge*

Morning Glory

This updated Kingfisher Butcher is a great fly for sea-trout shoaling in streamy water. It is also a great fly for rainbows on a day of sun and high white clouds.

Hook: *Size 8-14*
Thread: *Black*
Tail: *Kingfisher wing fibres or a bunch of bright-blue cock hackles*
Body: *Flat gold tinsel*
Wing: *White-tipped grey squirrel tail*
Hackle: *Hot-orange cock*

Haslam

An old Welsh sea-trout pattern to rely on. It
can be a great fly when the water is high and
clearing after a summer flood.

Hook: *Size 6-10*
Thread: *Black*
Tag: *Silver tinsel*
Tail: *Golden-pheasant topping feather*
Butt: *White wool, ostrich herl or*
fluorescent-orange floss
Body: *Flat silver tinsel*
Wing: *Hen-pheasant centre tail*
Horns: *Blue and yellow macaw fibres*
Hackle: *Blue jay*

Camasunary Killer

A loch sea-trout special that can be
devastatingly successful on a day with a
strong wind and goodish wave.

Hook: *Size 8-12*
Thread: *Black*
Tail: *Fluorescent-blue wool*
Body: *Rear half, fluorescent-blue wool;*
front half, fluorescent-red wool
Rib: *Oval silver*
Hackle: *Palmered long black cock*

Gold Butcher

A variation of the more famous Silver Butcher, this fly can be deadly during the day when the river is falling and clearing.

Hook: *Size 10-14*
Thread: *Black*
Tail: *Red ibis or swan dyed red*
Body: *Flat gold tinsel*
Rib: *Oval gold tinsel or gold wire*
Wing: *Blue mallard, crow wing or magpie tail feather*
Hackle: *Black*

Teal, Blue and Silver

One of the most famous of all sea-trout flies, the Teal, Blue and Silver is a killer on all rivers throughout the UK and Ireland. Fish a size 8 at night and sizes 10-14 during the day.

Hook: *Size 8-14*
Tail: *Golden-pheasant tippets*
Body: *Flat silver tinsel*
Rib: *Fine silver wire*
Wing: *Teal flank feather*
Hackle: *Bright-blue cock*

Thompson Terror

Invented by Bob Thompson, bailiff on the Border Esk, this fly, which looks like a bastardised Greenwell's Glory, is a brilliant pattern for sea-trout during the day.

Hook: Size 8-14 double
Thread: Pale primrose
Body: Pearl tinsel criss-crossed with the tying silk
Hackle: Greenwell saddle hackle with
shiny greenish centre

Dark Mackerel

One of the best sea-trout patterns for both river and loch, it seems most popular where waters carry a peat stain, such as in the north-west.

Hook: *Size 8-10*
Thread: *Black*
Tail: *Slim bunch of golden-pheasant tippet fibres*
Body: *Flat red lurex*
Body hackle: *Dark claret cock, tied sparse*
Rib: *Fine copper wire*
Wing: *Brown mallard*
Head hackle: *Longish dark-claret hen*

Peter Ross

Reputed to be one of the best sea-trout flies
ever devised, it is also a good small-fry
imitation, and should be fished on the point.

Hook: *8-14*
Tail: *Golden-pheasant tippets*
Body: *Rear half, silver tinsel; front half, red seal's fur*
Rib: *Oval silver tinsel*
Wing: *Barred teal breast feather fibres*
Hackle: *Black cock or hen*

Langholm Silver

Combine the hour before dark and newly
arrived sea-trout and you have the perfect
opportunity for tying on this fly, which
originated on the Border Esk.

Hook: *Size 8-12 singles and doubles*
Thread: *Black*
Tail: *Golden-pheasant tippets or topping*
Body: *Flat silver tinsel*
Wing: *Originally curlew; use strongly barred hen
pheasant or similar as a substitute*
Hackle: *Black hen or brown partridge*

Allrounder

When at a loss as to what to offer next,
reach for the Allrounder, a fly which has
everything a sea-trout is known to fancy.
Reputed to be at its best when fished in low
water from July onwards.

Hook: *Size 6-8 longshank*
Thread: *Black*
Tail: *Golden-pheasant topping*
Body: *Black seal's fur*
Rib: *Oval silver tinsel*
Wing: *Black squirrel overlaid with dyed red
squirrel and peacock sword herls*
Hackle: *Black cock*
Cheeks: *Jungle cock*

Heckham and Silver

A neglected old fly capable of doing great damage among shoals of newly arrived sea-trout lying in a fast stream.

Hook: *Size 8-12*
Thread: *Black*
Tail: *Golden-pheasant tippets*
Body: *Flat silver tinsel*
Rib: *Fine silver wire*
Wing: *White-tipped mallard feather*
Hackle: *Black cock or hen*

Alexandra

This ancient fly, once considered so deadly
on some brown trout waters that it was
banned, is an excellent pattern for
night-time sea-trout.

Hook: *Size 10-12*
Tail: *Red ibis or swan fibres dyed
red as a substitute*
Body: *Flat silver tinsel*
Rib: *Oval silver tinsel*
Hackle: *Black hen*
Wing: *Peacock sword herls, flanked either
side with swan fibres dyed red*

Colonel Downman

This old pattern is a great killer of sea-trout.
It is also sometimes tied with a wing of
light starling.

Hook: *Size 8-12*
Tail: *Teal fibres*
Body: *Black floss*
Rib: *Oval silver tinsel*
Hackle: *Black hen*
Wing: *Blue-barred jay feather*
Cheeks: *Jungle cock*

Watson's Fancy

An old Scottish loch and sea-trout pattern
that is still popular in its home country.

Hook: *Size 8-14*
Tail: *Small golden-pheasant crest feather*
Body: *Rear half, red seal's fur; front half,
black seal's fur*
Rib: *Silver tinsel*
Wing: *Crow wing with a small jungle
cock eye at either side*
Hackle: *Black hen*

River Trout

Here are the flies you need to catch the brownies of the river. Wet-flies, dry-flies and nymphs, they will serve you well wherever you fish.

Large Dark Olive

This large upwinged insect is one of the first ephemerids to make an appearance on the spring streams. Other hatches will come later in the year, these tending to be smaller and paler as the weather warms. The bigger, darker version appears again on some rivers during late September.

Hook: *Size 12-14*
Thread: *Olive*
Tail: *Slim bunch of hare's body guard hairs*
Body: *Dubbed hare's ear fur*
Hackle: *Sooty olive cock*

Nevamis Mayfly

Because this child of the chalkstreams floats
low on the surface, the ratio of rises to firm
hookings is considerably improved.

Hook: *Size 8 longshank*
Thread: *Brown*
Tail: *Three cock pheasant tail fibres*
Body: *Natural unbleached seal's fur*
Rib: *Fine oval gold tinsel*
Body hackle: *Palmered honey cock trimmed in
a taper to the tail*
Wing: *Pale-blue dun cock set upright with
a figure-of-eight lashing*
Hackle: *Furnace cock*

The Keeper's Nymph

This shrimpy imitation can be offered with
confidence to a winter grayling.

Hook: *Size 12-14*
Underbody: *Fine lead or copper wire*
Tail: *Fawny-brown grey squirrel fibres*
Body: *Red silk*
Rib: *Fine flat gold*
Back: *Woodpigeon primary feather herls*
Hackle: *Black cock divided into two equal bunches*
with the grey back herls

Bradshaw's Fancy

Results bear out the traditional thinking that this bright little grayling fly does best when fished late in the season. It can be used either wet or dry, and usually occupies pole position on the point.

Hook: Size 14-16
Thread: Purple
Tags: Crimson wool at head and tail
Body: Peacock herl
Hackle: Pale-blue dun hen. The original used Norwegian or hooded crow

Wylye Terror

An impression of the olive dun which is often
accepted without hesitation when more
realistic offerings have been shunned.

Hook: *Size 14-16*
Thread: *Olive*
Tail: *Honey dun cock fibres left long*
Body: *Undyed peacock quill*
Hackles: *Honey cock at the shoulder behind
a light blue cock at the head*

Pepper's Own

A dry-fly that has stood the test of time on all kinds of rivers as a general impression of a wide range of upwinged flies. Grayling fishers hold it in high regard, especially when it is tied very small.

Hook: *Size 14-16*
Thread: *Brown*
Tail: *Three strands of cock pheasant tail fibres*
Body: *Same strands wound*
Rib: *Red silk*
Hackles: *Two – honey grizzle behind natural red cock*

Endrick Spider

This drab little spider is one of the most
reliable all-rounders. Fish it on the point or
middle dropper on both stillwaters and rivers
at any time of the season.

Hook: *Size 12-14*
Thread: *Orange*
Tail: *Cock pheasant tail fibres*
Body: *Copper wire over-wound with cock
pheasant tail fibres*
Rib: *Silver or copper wire*
Hackle: *Grey partridge*

Bracken Clock

This ancient pattern gives of its best
when beetles and other terrestrials are
careless enough to fall from bankside bushes
into the water.

Hook: *Size 14*
Thread: *Black*
Body: *Bronze peacock herl*
Rib: *Red floss*
Hackle: *Cock pheasant neck feather which
is brown with black tips*

Goddard's Last Hope

This aptly named little fly will often turn the tables on a trout that has decided that caenis are the only thing worth lifting a fin for.

Hook: Size 18
Thread: Cream or yellow
Tail: Nylon microfibetts
Body: Grey or cream goose herl
Hackle: Cream, very short in the fibre

Partridge and Orange Bug

This effective grayling fly is usually offered on
the point below a big well-oiled Sedge on a
dropper fixed a couple of feet away.

Hook: *Size 10-14*
Thread: *Black*
Underbody: *Lead foil strips fixed on top of the shank*
Body: *Orange floss*
Back: *Grey feather herls*
Rib: *Fine gold wire over body and back*
Hackle: *Brown partridge fibres tied as a beard*

Bustard

One to tie on when the bats and owls come out to play. Fish it as a single fly across the surface of the pools. Be prepared for some surprisingly large trout.

Hook: *Size 10-12*
Thread: *Brown*
Body: *Rusty brown seal's fur or substitute*
Rib: *Flat gold tinsel*
Wing: *Hen pheasant*
Hackle: *Ginger*

White-Head Nymph

This superb little nymph enjoyed a devastatingly successful debut when Poland's Adam Sikora used it to gain second place when the World Championships were staged on the Welsh Dee.

Hook: *Size 10*
Thread: *Fawn*
Body: *Copper-coloured wool over a lead wire underbody*
Thorax: *Cream wool*
Head: *Fawn thread*

Skues' Iron Blue

One of the best possible patterns to employ
when attempting to imitate either the
emerging insect or the full-blown dun.

Hook: *Size 14-16*
Thread: *Claret or crimson*
Tail: *Two or three strands of white or pale-blue dun
cock hackle fibres*
Body: *Dubbed mole's fur*
Hackle: *Dark-blue dun*

Aphid

High-summer trout often stir themselves to take one of these tiny bugs when other, more substantial, morsels are ignored. Fish the artificial on a long leader and fine tippet.

Hook: *Size 14-16*
Thread: *Green*
Tail: *Blue-dun cock tied short*
Body: *Pale-green floss or seal's fur*
Hackle: *Blue-dun cock*

Silver Twist

Use in either wet or dry versions for winter grayling, especially should the day be blessed with a mid-day hatch of olives. Add a lead wire underbody and it becomes a most useful nymph.

Hook: *Size 14-16*
Thread: *Black*
Body: *Natural rabbit underfur (blue-grey)*
Rib: *Oval silver*
Hackle: *Natural blue dun*

Cran Swallow

This fly, from the Border streams, produces its fair share of fish whatever the identity of the hatch of natural insects.

Hook: *Size 14-16*
Thread: *Waxed primrose Pearsall's Gossamer silk*
Body: *Tying silk*
Wing: *Coot or crow tied low over the body*
Hackle: *One turn of starling in front of the wing*

Dark Watchet

This reliable northern wet-fly imitates the
emerging nymphs and drowned duns and
spinners of the iron blue.

Hook: *Size 14*
Body: *Orange and purple tying silks twisted together
and thinly dubbed with mole's fur*
Hackle: *Jackdaw throat feather*

Elk-Hair Caddis

One of the best sedge imitations on both stillwaters and rivers. In tumbling streams the deerhair wing and palmered hackle help keep the fly afloat.

Hook: *Size 14*
Body: *SLF MC 10, or similar green synthetic dubbing ribbed with short-fibred brown cock hackle*
Wing: *Natural elk or deerhair with butts clipped to small head*

Borsten

This impression of a cased caddis deserves
pride of place when fishing for both winter
grayling and early-season trout, particularly
after a flood has dislodged a supply of
naturals from their not-so-safe havens
among the stones.

Hook: *Size 10-12 standard or longshank*
Body: *Olive, brown and black cock hackles*
tightly wound over an underbody of
lead or copper wire and trimmed
Head: *Long and formed with the tying thread*

Winter Brown

A reliable imitation of the small thin needle flies that appear as early as February on the northern streams. A great taker of early trout, it is also a wise choice for an October grayling cast.

Hook: Size 12-14
Body: Red Pearsall's No 11a
Hackle: Under covert from a woodcock's wing
Head: Peacock herl

Mini Wulff

Although much smaller than the natural insect, this little dry-fly – usually fished two on a leader – is at its best when cast in front of trout searching for the hatching Mayfly duns.

Hook: *Size 12-14*
Thread: *Black*
Tail: *Grey squirrel*
Body: *Blue rabbit underfur*
Hackle: *Lemon-dyed grizzle cock*
Wing: *Grey squirrel tail*

Pale Evening Dun

One to rely on when the natural insect
hatches off the more leisurely moving parts
of the river in July and August.

Hook: *Size 14-16*
Thread: *White*
Tail: *Cream cock hackle fibres*
Body: *Grey goose herl doubled and
re-doubled at thorax*
Hackle: *Cream cock*

Spent Gnat

Many knowledgeable Irish fishers pin their faith on this fly at Mayfly time. It has the distinct advantage over many other imitations in that it takes fish feeding on the spent fly during daylight hours.

Hook: *Size 8-10*
Thread: *Brown*
Tail: *Four dyed black pheasant-tail fibres*
Body: *Natural raffia*
Rib: *Fine oval gold tinsel*
Body hackle: *Short grizzle or badger*
Wing: *Dark-blue dun hackle tips with a long blue dun cock wound, and then divided into the spent position*

Pheasant Tail

One for summer evenings when the
blue-winged olive spinners start to dance
above the darkening stream.

Hook: *Size 14-16*
Thread: *Orange*
Tail: *Honey dun fibres*
Body: *Fibres torn from a
reddish/chestnut pheasant tail*
Rib: *Fine gold wire*
Hackle: *Rusty dun cock*

Black Gnat

Use this one when the real insect or anything small and black is on the water.

Hook: *Size 16-22*
Thread: *Black*
Body: *Fine black fur*
Wing: *White poly yarn*
Hackle: *Black cock*

Early Brown

An essential pattern for more northerly streams, particularly those with a population of the stonefly, of which this old pattern is a reliable imitation.

Hook: *Size 14-16*
Thread: *Red*
Body: *Brown seal's fur very lightly dubbed*
Hackle: *Coot, palmered at the shoulder*

Williams' Favourite

This old pattern bears out the sound advice
that whenever things get difficult you can do
no better than tie on a small black fly.

Hook: *Size 10-16*
Thread: *Black*
Tail: *Black cock hackle fibres*
Rib: *Oval silver*
Body: *Black floss or tying thread*
Hackle: *Black cock or hen*

Black Sedge

Small black sedges skittering across the surface of fast-flowing streams are a common sight on summer evenings. Treat the fly with floatant, and fish it singly to rising fish.

Hook: *Size 12*
Thread: *Black*
Rib: *Gold wire*
Body: *Black seal's fur*
Wings: *Crow secondary tied low over the body*
Hackle: *Dark Greenwell*

Shadow Mayfly

Although designed primarily for the chalkstreams of the South, this great bumble of a Mayfly performs equally well on more northerly waters lucky enough to support hatches of the big ephemerid.

Hook: *Size 10-12 longshank*
Thread: *Black or brown*
Body: *None as such, grizzle hackles closely wound*
Wing: *Ginger hackles clipped at the tip*

Caddis Larva

This caddis imitation can be fished on stillwaters or tumbling streams from the first day of the season to the last.

Hook: *Size 12-16*
Thread: *Brown*
Underbody: *Fine lead wire*
Body: *Golden-pheasant tail feather fibres*
Rib: *Gold wire*
Hackle: *Brown partridge wound in front of a small dubbing of hare's ear fur*
Head: *Peacock herl*

Black Spider

This old classic will take fish from the first
day of the season to the last whenever
anything small and dark is hatching.

Hook: *Size 14-16*
Body: *Brown silk well-waxed to near black,*
Pearsall's No 17
Hackle: *Starling neck feather*

Iron Blue Spider

Given the choice, the natural iron blue likes to hatch on a cold and blustery day, an unusual preference for early-season stream-fishers of Wales, the north, and western parts of the country.

Hook: *Size 14*
Thread: *Crimson*
Tip: *Tying thread*
Body: *Mole's fur*
Hackle: *Inside of a moorhen's wing*

Something and Nothing

This down-at-heel Coachman is not one for those who look for close imitation in their flies but, when the trout prove to be difficult, this tatty killer is a first-choice pattern on both rivers and stillwaters.

Hook: *Size 8-14*
Thread: *Brown*
Body: *Peacock herl wound over a lead wire underbody (optional) then clipped short*
Wing: *Short stub of any white feather herl*
Hackle: *Brown hen trimmed to form a collar*

White Grizzly

An effective imitation of the pale watery, it is
often the only thing that trout will look at
after the annual binge on Mayflies.

Hook: *Size 14-16*
Thread: *Orange*
Tail: *Honey hackle fibres*
Body: *White rabbit dyed a pale honey*
Rib: *Yellow floss*
Hackles: *Grizzle cock with a pale badger cock
wound through it*

John Titmouse

This unusual fly was designed as a counter measure for those infuriating times when grayling come rushing at the fly, only to reject it after the merest peck.

Hook: *Size 16-18*
Tail: *White hackle fibres*
Body: *Peacock herl*
Wing: *A slim bunch of mallard breast feather fibres sloping out over the eye*
Hackle: *Black cock*

Kite's Imperial

Invented by the late Oliver Kite as an olive imitation for spring on the River Teifi, this dry-fly works well on rivers throughout the country.

Hook: *Size 14-18*
Thread: *Purple*
Tail: *Honey cock hackle fibres*
Rib: *Fine gold wire*
Body: *Grey feather fibres doubled at the thorax*
Hackle: *Honey dun or bronze blue dun (Andalusian) cock*

Balloon Caddis

This modern imitation is regarded by many
to be the most effective adult sedge imitation
yet devised. Offer it singly on a long,
fine leader.

Hook: *Size 14-16*
Thread: *To match body colour*
Body: *Dubbed grey or green to match the
natural sedge*
Wing: *Natural coastal deerhair*
Thorax cover: *Yellow ethafoam*

Black Magic

Simplicity itself to tie, this little gem of a fly can be offered on waters running and still with confidence, especially when anything small and dark is hatching.

Hook: *Size 14-18*
Thread: *Black*
Body: *Tying thread*
Thorax: *Peacock herl*
Hackle: *Black hen*

Renegade

A great fly when fishing for trout lying in fast and broken streams. The white hackle provides a useful marker for those with less-than-perfect sight.

Hook: *Size 10-12*
Thread: *Black*
Tip: *Flat gold tinsel*
Rear hackle: *Brown or natural red cock*
Body: *Peacock herl*
Front hackle: *White cock*

Black Pensioner

Anyone who has difficulty in spotting a
dry-fly bobbing along at more than a few
yards away should try this pattern, which is
usually accepted when hawthorn flies or any
darkish terrestrials are on the water.

Hook: *Size 12*
Thread: *Black*
Tail: *Black cock hackle fibres*
Body: *Black feather fibre*
Rib: *Fine gold wire*
Wing: *White mink or goat hair tied as a post*
Hackle: *Black cock hackle wound around the
wing roots*

Double Legs

This unusual fly is deadly on both rivers and small stillwaters when cast to visible fish. Add more weight near the head and it becomes the perfect tool for winkling out those canny residents reluctant to budge from their holts beneath the roots.

Hook: *Size 10*
Thread: *Brown*
Head: *4 mm gold bead*
Body: *Rabbit underfur*
Hackle: *Grey partridge wound at head and tail*

Dove Bug

When grayling go off the Killer Bug and all
things beige, this is the one to tie on. It is
particularly useful when grayling are huddled
in deep holes following a big winter flood.

Hook: *Size 10-12*
Thread: *Brown*
Body: *Copper or lead wire underbody.*
Rear half, orange and pink seal's fur;
front half, orange and brown seal's fur
Rib: *Gold or copper wire*

Greenwell's Spider

Fish this one with total confidence when and wherever any of the olive clan is hatching.

Hook: *Size 14*
Thread: *Waxed yellow silk*
Rib: *Gold wire*
Hackle: *Long coch-y-bonddu or
furnace hen fibres*

Priest

This sparkling little fly can be excellent when put before a grayling, especially when the water is still carrying colour after a winter flood. Dressed on a larger size, it can be good for sea-trout shoaling in a quick stream.

Hook: *Size 14*
Thread: *Black*
Tail: *Red wool or slip of dyed red feather*
Body: *Flat silver tinsel*
Rib: *Silver wire*
Hackle: *Badger hen*

Killer Bug

A loose impression of a shrimp or larva of some sort, this bug can be deadly when trout and grayling can be seen lying in clear water. Takes are signalled by the flash of a mouth or by the fish suddenly moving.

Hook: *Size 10-14*
Thread: *Brown or fine copper wire*
Body: *At least two layers of wire covered with Chadwick's 477 darning wool. Use light beige wool as a substitute*

Green Lurex Nymph

When reservoirs and streams are struck by a prolonged drought and the trout head for the cool of the deeps, that is the time to tie on this little sparkler, which the trout probably take for a darting beetle.

Hook: *Size 10-14*
Thread: *Black*
Body: *Lead-foil underbody covered with bright-green lurex*
Head: *Peacock herl*
Hackle: *Soft brown hen*

Orange Otter

Try this bright little dry-fly when grayling have refused more traditionally hackled patterns. Tied on a size 18, it will often deceive the pickiest of fish.

Hook: *Size 14-18*
Thread: *Orange*
Tail: *Natural red cock hackle fibres*
Body: *Hot-orange seal's fur*
Hackle: *Natural red tied in the middle of the body*

Goldbead Hare's Ear

This pattern is so effective the season through that there is a danger of it being used to the exclusion of almost anything else in the fly box. On streams, it can be fished on the 'dead drift' or twitched slowly through the deep holes. On small stillwaters, it is often taken as it falls through the water. A first-choice fly for stalking large rainbows.

Hook: *Size 10-14*
Thread: *Brown*
Tail: *Tuft of hare's body fur guard hairs*
Rib: *Flat gold or pearl tinsel*
Head: *Gold bead*

Duck's Dun

This Charles Jardine imitation of a hatching dun has relegated many old favourites to a forgotten corner of the fly box. Just change the size of the fly and shade to match the hatch of the day.

Hook: *Size 14-20*
Thread: *Primrose yellow*
Tail: *Grizzle cock hackle fibres*
Body: *Pale-yellow-olive antron or similar*
Wing: *Two cul-de-canard plumes tied back to back*
Hackle: *Blue dun wound through the thorax area and clipped in a 'V' underneath*

Grayling Fiddler

One to have in the box when grayling turn up
their noses at the usual offerings. This
unusually dressed pattern rarely fails to
deceive even the most difficult fish.

Hook: *Size 16-18*
Thread: *Brown*
Body: *Dubbed red wool or fluorescent floss wound
from half-way around the bend to the eye*
Hackle: *Short-fibred grizzle cock*

Shrymp

One of those bugs that are all things edible to trout and big grayling. Expect great things of it in both rivers and stillwaters.

Hook: *Size 8-12*
Thread: *Brown or olive*
Underbody: *Lead wire*
Body and thorax: *Seal's fur. A blend of five parts green, four of brown and one part fluorescent pink*
Rib: *Flat silver over abdomen only*
Thorax cover: *Flue from the base of a black feather doubled and redoubled*

John Storey

One of those useful dry-flies that, while representing nothing in particular, is readily taken for a wide range of insects. It revels in a quick and bubbling stream.

Hook: *Size 10-14*
Thread: *Black*
Body: *Peacock herl*
Wing: *Pale partridge, teal or mallard breast feather tied advanced over the eye*
Hackle: *Dark-red cock*

Griffith's Gnat

This little palmer has crossed the Atlantic
most successfully. Use it when midges are
hatching on still or running waters, and the
trout are sipping in anything tiny and
unidentifiable.

Hook: *Size 16-22*
Thread: *Black micro*
Body: *Peacock herl*
Hackle: *Short-fibred grizzle*

Snipe and Purple

Tied to imitate the nymph of the iron-blue dun, this little spider takes some beating when used in its original role on rain-fed rivers.

Hook: *Size 14*
Body: *Purple silk*
Hackle: *A dark feather from a snipe's wing*

Chatsworth Bug

Those who fail with bead-headed bugs should give this one a try. More often than not the reason for the disappointment is that the speed of the stream has not been taken into account, keeping them off the bottom, where they do their best work.

Hook: *Size 10-14 standard or longshank*
Thread: *Brown*
Tail: *Short pearl Krystal Flash*
Body: *Dubbed pine squirrel*
Rib: *Gold wire*
Collar (optional): *Green or orange fluorescent floss or dubbing*
Head: *Originally a gold bead, but copper and silver make excellent patterns*

Partridge and Orange

With few equals as a nymph-suggesting
pattern for fast-flowing streams at any
time of the season, it has also accounted for
some very big stillwater rainbows when
dressed 'short' on size 8 hooks. Ribbed with
a single pheasant tail fibre, it is an excellent
pattern when sedges are hatching on the
big reservoirs.

Hook: *Size 12-14*
Body: *Orange silk*
Hackle: *Two turns of brown partridge*

Beacon Beige

The original pattern was tied during the First
World War and this fly is considered one of
the best olive dun imitations to use.

Hook: *Size 12-18*
Thread: *Yellow*
Tail: *Plymouth Rock (grizzle) cock hackle fibres*
Body: *Well-marked stripped peacock eye quill*
Hackle: *Plymouth Rock (grizzle) cock with a
red Indian game-cock wound through*

Adams

This North American standard utility pattern
and dun imitation is probably one of the most
popular – and useful – dry-flies in the world.

Hook: *Size 14-16*
Thread: *Grey*
Tail: *Grizzle hackle fibres*
Body: *Blue-grey dubbed wool or fur*
Wings: *Two grizzle hackles tied upright*
Hackle: *Red and grizzle cock wound together*

Grey Duster

An excellent dry-fly, this is a killing pattern for trout and grayling. The smaller sizes are useful midge and caenis imitations; the medium sizes are a general stonefly imitation and the bigger sizes can represent a moth.

Hook: *10-14*
Tail (optional): *Badger cock hackle fibres*
Body: *Blue-grey rabbit fur*
Hackle: *Badger cock*

F Fly

This easy-to-tie fly is deadly as a midge, dun or emerger imitator.

Hook: *Size 12-20*
Thread: *To match the body colour*
Body: *Olive feather fibre*
Wing: *A bunch of cul-de-canard feathers*

Clipped Coachman

Once tried, this beetle-like bug is likely to be a firm favourite when fishing rough streams for either trout or grayling. The white tuft acts as a useful sighting aid when stalking fish in small stillwaters.

Hook: *Size 12-14*
Thread: *Black*
Body: *Peacock herl weighted with copper or lead wire as an option*
Hackle: *Brown hen*
Wing: *White feather fibres trimmed to a stub*

Woodcock and Hare's Ear

A golden oldie well worth an extended
wetting when small dark sedges are on the
water.

Hook: *Size 12-14*
Tip: *Flat gold*
Tail: *Brown mallard fibres*
Body: *Dark hare's ear*
Rib: *Fine oval gold tinsel*
Wing: *Slips taken from a woodcock wing quill*
Hackle: *Body fibres picked out*

Stillwater
Trout

In this section are flies for wild waters and man-made fisheries. Each fly has a well-earned reputation.

J.C. Claret Emerger

The J.C. Claret Emerger works well during a midge hatch or when the fish are concentrating on unidentifiable small stuff on the surface.

Hook: *Size 12-16*
Thread: *Black or claret*
Tag: *Pearl mylar*
Body: *Claret seal's fur*
Rib: *Pearl mylar*
Wing: *Jungle cock*
Thorax: *As the body*
Hackle: *Natural red/brown cock*

Blae and Black

An excellent chironomid imitation, the Blae and Black is a great favourite on Irish loughs during the spring duckfly hatch.

Hook: *Size 10-14*
Thread: *Black*
Tail: *Golden-pheasant tippets*
Body: *Black floss*
Rib: *Silver wire*
Wing: *Starling*
Hackle: *Black*

Hare's Face Nymph

One to fish very slowly on a long leader when
nothing stirs. A small version is highly
effective when offered close to the surface
during a hatch of pale chironomids or sedges.

Hook: *Size 8-10*
Thread: *Brown*
Tail: *Small bunch of white cock hackle fibres*
Body: *From the hare's face, ginger and blue*
dun fibres mixed
Rib: *Medium copper wire*
Thorax: *As the body*
Wing case: *Mottled brown hen or*
turkey feather

Wee Peter

This cut-down Peter Ross works well during a hatch of chironomids. Fished on the point, it will take fish on difficult days in high summer.

Hook: *Size 12*
Thread: *Black*
Body: *Two-thirds flat silver tinsel behind front third of scarlet fluorescent wool*
Hackle: *Black hen wound as a collar*

Ant

This is a fly that makes perhaps a
once-a-year outing but, when the trout are
locked on to the tiny insects, no other
pattern will fit the bill.

Hook: *Size 14-16*
Thread: *Black*
Body: *Black ethafoam trimmed to shape and
fixed at the centre of the hook*
Hackle: *Red hackle wound in the central crease*

Silver Dabbler

This Sheelin special is well worth its place on the leader at any time of the season, but especially when the trout are picking off small fry.

Hook: *Size 10-14*
Thread: *Red*
Tail: *Cock pheasant tail fibres*
Body: *Claret seal's fur*
Body rib: *Medium flat silver tinsel*
Body hackle: *Palmered ginger cock and two full turns at the head*
Hackle rib: *Fine oval silver following the flat tinsel turns*
Head hackle: *Bronze mallard fibres swept back*

Challoner

Although abandoned by many stillwater fishers in favour of more modern dressings, this old pattern will take some beating when yellow-bodied sedges are hatching. It is effective on days of a good wave.

Hook: *Size 12-14*
Thread: *Yellow*
Tail: *Red feather fibres*
Body: *Amber or yellow seal's fur*
Rib: *Oval gold tinsel*
Body: *Hen pheasant wing quill*
Hackle: *Brown hen*

Bi-Visible Dapper

This one fits the bill nicely when there's a good wind and rolling wave. It can also be fished on the bob of a three-fly cast.

Hook: *Size 6-12*
Thread: *Black*
Tail: *Black cock hackle fibres*
Body: *None*
Hackles: *Black and white cock hackles in bands ending with black at the eye*
Head: *Black*

Copper Squirrel

This little bug is the one to tie on when flies
bearing the more usual gold beads have lost
their charms.

Hook: *Size 12-14*
Bead: *2 mm copper*
Thread: *Brown*
Body: *Grey squirrel fur*
Rib: *Fine gold wire*
Hackle: *Brown partridge tied
behind the bead*

Baddow Special

An excellent general-purpose pattern
probably taken for a damsel larva. Fish
it with confidence on stillwaters large
and small.

Hook: *Size 8-10 longshank*
Thread: *Black*
Tail: *Fluorescent-lime wool*
Body: *Peacock herl*
Rib: *Fine copper wire*
Hackle: *Long white cock*

Burleigh

Although primarily designed to imitate the
lake olive, this is one to try when
green-bodied buzzers or sedges
are hatching off.

Hook: *Size 12-16*
Thread: *Pale green*
Tail: *Two or three golden-pheasant tippet
fibres left long*
Body: *Medium green wool or seal's fur tied thin and
tapered from head to tail*
Rib: *Oval gold tinsel or wire*
Wing: *Starling or teal wing feather*
Hackle: *Pale ginger*

Muddled Daddy

A superb pattern for autumn fishing in a big
wave on all stillwaters. Fish it quickly on a
floating line and be prepared for exciting
follows and swirls!

Hook: *Size 10-12*
Thread: *Black*
Body: *Hare's fur ribbed with oval gold*
Legs: *Knotted pheasant tail fibres*
Head: *Natural coastal deerhair*

Humpy

This unsinkable dry-fly is earning a quite remarkable reputation as a taker of good trout on the Irish loughs during Mayfly time when the more conventional artificials have failed.

Hook: *Size 10-14*
Thread: *Yellow*
Tail: *Moose body hair*
Body: *Natural deerhair over dubbed
light-yellow fur*
Hackle: *Grizzle*
Wing: *The tips of the deerhair used
for the body*

Watson's Bumble

One for a dark day and a big wave. Regarded
by many lough fishers as a rival for the
Claret Bumble when they are looking for a fly
to fill that all-important top-dropper position.

Hook: *Size 8-14*
Thread: *Black*
Body: *Rear-half, red seal's fur;*
front-half, black seal's fur
Rib: *Fine oval or flat silver tinsel*
Hackle: *Black cock palmered along the body behind*
three or four turns of blue jay
Eyes: *Jungle-cock*

Melvin Octopus

This great straggle of a fly has a reputation for tempting Lough Melvin's trout feasting on the emerging Mayfly.

Hook: *Size 8-12*
Thread: *Brown*
Tag: *Two turns flat gold tinsel*
Tail: *Tuft of fluorescent-yellow floss (Glo-Brite 11)*
Body: *Golden-olive seal's fur*
Body hackles: *Green-olive and golden-olive*
Rib: *Fine oval gold*
Head hackle: *Golden-pheasant yellow rump feather*

Leven Ghost

Reach for this American-looking lure
when fry and perch are milling around
the weedbeds.

Hook: *Size 8 longshank*
Thread: *Black*
Body: *Orange floss*
Rib: *Narrow flat silver*
Hackle: *White marabou tied as a throat hackle
reaching the hook bend*
Wing: *Four peacock herls with two golden-pheasant
crest feathers over and two olive cock hackles
on each side*
Cheeks: *Jungle cock*

Silver Tip

One to try with confidence when anything small, black and unidentifiable is on the water. It can do great things in early season fished on the edge of a ripple when trout are picking off tiny midges.

Hook: *Size 14*
Thread: *Black*
Tip: *Flat silver*
Body: *Magpie or any black feather herl*
Hackle: *Black hen*

Leonard's Hatching Duckfly

There are times when this unusual pattern is preferred to more conventional offerings during a hatch of chironomids.

Hook: *Size 12*
Thread: *Brown*
Body: *Flat silver overlaid with clear PVC*
Wing: *White-tipped grey squirrel tail*
Thorax: *Ostrich herl, three turns of black behind three turns of red*
Head: *Red varnish*

Pearly Bibio

There are few big waters where the Bibio fails to claim a regular share of the bag. This updated version is earning the distinction of out-fishing its illustrious ancestor as a top-dropper fly when the sun breaks through the clouds.

Hook: Size 12
Thread: Black
Body: Pearl tinsel either side of a red or orange
fluorescent wool band
Hackle: Long black cock
Rib: Fine silver wire

Near-Perfect Buzzer

Resist the temptation to retrieve the nymph
at anything above a snail's pace.

Hook: *Size 10-14 Partridge K14ST*
Thread: *Black*
Body: *Peacock quill, stripped and varnished*
Cheeks: *Fluorescent-orange floss*
Thorax: *Peacock herl*
Hackle: *One turn grey hen*

Daddy Longlegs

While usually offered as a dry-fly, this
gangle-legged imitation can be even deadlier
when fished on a slow-sinking line.

Hook: *Size 8-10 longshank*
Thread: *Brown*
Body: *Natural raffia, foam or cock pheasant tail fibres*
Rib: *Brown thread*
Legs: *Six or eight knotted cock pheasant tail fibres*
Wings: *Cree hackle points*
Hackle: *Pale ginger cock*

Cinnamon Sparkle Caddis

A great fly for stillwater and stream when sedges are about.

Hook: *Size 16*
Tail: *Yellow sparkle yarn (Lureflash antron body wool)*
Body: *SLF MC 11 or similar cinnamon synthetic dubbing*
Wing: *Deerhair, natural or dyed grey, with butts clipped to a small head*

Bog Fly

Originally tied for Irish sea-trout, this beetle-like fly works well with brown trout on windy days when the heather fly is blown on to upland lakes in late summer.

Hook: *Size 10-14*
Thread: *Black*
Body: *Black ostrich herl*
Rib: *Fine oval silver*
Wing: *Crow outside slips of red swan*
Hackle: *Scarlet cock*

Deerhair Dapper

This large but lightweight dapping fly doesn't need a gale to keep it skipping across the waves. Originally designed for sea-trout and salmon, it is equally good for both brown trout and rainbows when they come up to feed on daddy longlegs.

Hook: *Size 8, 6 or 4 low-water salmon iron*
Thread: *Brown*
Body and hackles: *Spun natural deerhair.*
The body is trimmed short and the fibres at either end left untouched

Black Joe

One for an early stillwater when small black chironomids are hatching. The stronger the wind and the bigger the wave the better. It gives of its best when fished on the point.

Hook: *Size 14-16 singles and doubles*
Thread: *Black*
Body: *Rear-half, fluorescent-red floss or wool;*
front-half, black ostrich herl
Hackle: *Black hen*

Big Grey

A reliable general-purpose pattern that excels during hatches of early-season olives. Dressed with a pale-yellow or olive body, it is most acceptable when trout are feeding on lighter-coloured insects.

Hook: *Size 12*
Thread: *Grey or black*
Body: *Dark hare's ear or black poly dubbing*
Hackle: *Palmered grey grizzle, clipped flush with the body underneath*

Appetiser

This excellent general-purpose lure is
extremely effective medicine when trout are
concentrating on fry. Tie it as a tandem when
the small fish are three or more inches long.

Hook: *Size 8 longshank*
Thread: *Black*
Tail: *Mixture of green and orange cock hackle fibres
and mallard breast feather fibres*
Body: *White chenille*
Rib: *Oval silver tinsel*
Wing: *White marabou with natural grey squirrel over*
Throat hackle: *As for tail*

Kingfisher Butcher

This no-holds-barred attractor can be an outstanding fly for both stillwater brownies and rainbows on a sunny day. Although rarely used in the role, it is a first-rate point fly for sea-trout in a dark or peat-stained loch.

Hook: *Size 10-12*
Thread: *Black*
Tail: *Bright-blue feather or hackle fibres*
Body: *Flat gold tinsel*
Rib: *Fine gold tinsel or wire*
Wing: *Blue mallard or crow*
Throat hackle: *Hot-orange cock*

Green Midge

An excellent dry-fly when trout are rising to the adult green buzzer. Fish it on its own or in partnership with a small green Buzzer on either point or dropper of a two-fly leader.

Hook: *Size 14-16*
Thread: *Yellow*
Body: *Bright-green goose herl*
Hackles: *Cropped grizzle cock palmered through the herl and a larger one at the head*

Cock Robin

This traditional Irish lough pattern is a good
fly for both point or middle dropper when
lake olives are hatching.

Hook: *Size 10-14*
Thread: *Black*
Tail: *Bronze mallard fibres*
Body: *In two halves: golden-olive seal's fur
behind red seal's fur*
Rib: *Oval gold tinsel*
Wing: *Bronze mallard*
Hackle: *Natural red game*

Concoction

Rainbows find this sedgy-looking fly very much to their liking throughout the season, especially when it occupies the prime top dropper and point positions. It works best on a bright and breezy day.

Hook: *Size 8-10*
Thread: *Green*
Body: *Seal's fur, green behind red*
Wing: *Light hen pheasant wing*
Hackle: *Ginger*

Black Wormfly

A great fly for the early-season bank-fisher who shuns the use of lures. Fish it on a leader up to 25 ft long and retrieve it at a snail's pace. For optimum results fish a couple of small dark Buzzers on droppers spaced at four-feet intervals.

Hook: *Size 10-12 longshank*
Thread: *Black*
Body: *Bronze peacock herl with bands of green fluorescent floss at tail and centre. A weighted underbody is optional.*
Rib: *Fine silver tinsel*
Hackles: *Longish black hen or cock*

McLeod's Olive

An old stager regarded by many Scottish fishers as a first-choice pattern when olives are hatching.

Hook: *Size 12-14*
Thread: *Pale olive or yellow*
Tail: *Tippets or hen hackle fibres dyed a greyish olive*
Tag: *Two turns flat gold tinsel*
Body: *Medium olive-green wool or mohair*
Wing: *Starling secondary slips*

Green Beast

A pattern every fisher of small stillwaters should have. Originally tied to imitate aquatic larvae, it's an excellent fish-taker in those fisheries 'blessed' with heavy weed growth or green algae.

Hook: *Size 8 longshank*
Thread: *Green*
Tail: *Green cock hackle fibres*
Body: *Bright-green floss silk tied to a carrot shape over a base of fine lead wire*
Rib: *Fine silver wire*
Hackle: *Brown partridge*

Loch Ordie

Although generally regarded purely as a dapping fly for sea-trout and salmon, this bushy fly performs equally well when trickled across the waves for both brown trout and rainbows in the final weeks of the season.

Hook: *Size 6-12 longshank*
Thread: *Brown*
Hackles: *A choice of black, red-brown, ginger or cree hackles. Wind on as many cock hackles of one colour as the hook will hold. Finish off with two longer-fibred white cock hackles at the head*

Alder

When trout are 'on' the natural insect they will accept the artificial with relish. But, be warned – if the first trout you offer it to refuses, replace it with something else.

Hook: *Size 10-12*
Thread: *Black*
Body: *Peacock herl*
Wing: *Brown speckled hen*
Hackle: *Black cock*

Texas Rose Muddler

It would have amused the late Dick Walker to hear that his fly is amazingly effective when scratched across the surface during a hatch of Mayfly on a small stillwater.

Hook: *Size 8 longshank*
Thread: *Yellow or orange*
Body: *Orange floss silk*
Rib: *Fine oval silver*
Wing: *Yellow bucktail*
Head: *Spun and clipped natural deerhair*

Wet Daddy

When the daddy is about – and even when it isn't – fish this big fly on a slow-sinking line and retrieve in long, steady draws.

Hook: *Size 10-12 longshank*
Thread: *Black*
Body: *Natural raffia*
Body hackle: *Palmered red cock at the front part of the body*
Rib: *Fine gold wire*
Hackle: *Large brown partridge and a golden-pheasant tippet feather*

Wormfly

When crept along the bottom or used to scratch the surface on a windy day, this old stager – getting on for 150 years old – will succeed where more modern patterns fail. Dressed on a leaded longshank hook, it is an excellent point fly for those stillwater anglers who shun the use of lures.

Hook: *Size 10-14 in tandem or size 10 longshank*
Thread: *Black*
Tail: *Red wool*
Body: *Bronze peacock herl*
Hackle: *Natural red hen or coch-y-bondhu*

Poxy Buzzer

One of the best of the modern Buzzers, this pattern should be allowed to drift round on the wind or retrieved ultra slowly.

Hook: *Size 10-12*
Body: *Black floss or thread*
Rib: *Fluorescent red thread*
Thorax: *Black thread with orange T-shirt paint wing buds. All coated with clear epoxy*

Big Foot

This simple pattern can be extremely deadly when snails head the menu for the day. Treat with floatant and allow the imitation to drift around on the ripple.

Hook: *Size 10-12*
Thread: *Black*
Body: *Peacock herl twisted into a rope*
Back: *Yellow ethafoam*

York's Special

One to reach for when the heather flies are
blown off the hillsides. Named after a
travelling fly-dresser who sold his creations
to the fly-fishers of North Wales.

Hook: *Size 10-14*
Thread: *Black*
Tail: *Red swan or goose*
Body: *Peacock herl*
Hackle: *Coch-y-bonddu*

Olive Fraser Nymph

This modern stillwater nymph can be fished with confidence when either olive chironomids or greenish sedges are hatching. Fish it on a long leader, and allow it to drift round on the wind, aided by the slowest of retrieves.

Hook: *Size 12-14 longshank*
Thread: *Olive*
Tail: *Olive-dyed hen pheasant tail fibres*
Body: *As tail, ribbed with green fluorescent floss*
Thorax: *Mix of olive seal's fur and hare's body fur*
Thorax cover and legs: *Olive-dyed pheasant tail fibres*

When All Else Fails Nymph

One for pitching in front of large trout cruising around in a clear stillwater. The white deerhair head is a great help when trying to spot the take in deep water.

Hook: *Size 12-14*
Thread: *Black*
Body: *Lead wire*
Head: *Tuft of white deerhair*

White-Hackled Invicta

This is one of those enigmatic patterns which does great things for some and nothing for others. It gives of its best on a day of big waves and lowering skies.

Hook: *Size 8-10*
Thread: *Brown*
Tail: *Golden-pheasant crest*
Body: *Yellow seal's fur*
Rib: *Gold wire*
Body hackle: *Natural light red*
Wing: *Hen pheasant tail*
Hackle: *Long white hen*

Shipman's Buzzer

Invented by match-fisherman Dave Shipman,
this fly is deadly when the trout are taking
the emerging insects.

Hook: *Size 12-14*
Tail and breathers: *White antron*
Body: *Seal's fur to match colour of hatch*
Rib: *Oval gold tinsel or wire*

Damsel

An excellent fly throughout the season, the Damsel should be fished with an erratic retrieve to imitate the agile natural.

Hook: *Size 8-12*
Thread: *Yellow*
Tail: *Olive marabou*
Body: *Dubbed marabou*
Rib: *Pearl mylar*
Hackle: *Grey partridge dyed olive*

Shuttlecock Hare's Ear Buzzer

A deadly pattern wherever dark buzzers are hatching. Cover individual rises or merely cast out and wait for the trout to find it.

Hook: *Size 10-16*
Silk: *To match body colour*
Tail: *Twisted strands of pearl Crystal Flash*
Body: *Hare's ear*
Wing: *Four plumes of cul-de-canard, brought over thorax and tied in at head*

Black and Peacock Spider

Tom Iven's B&P Spider is an effective all-rounder that takes fish at all depths. Probably best when fished slow and deep in early season or close to the surface when the trout are feeding on snails.

Hook: *Size 8-12*
Thread: *Black*
Body: *Peacock herl*
Hackle: *Sparse black hen*

Black Pennell

A standard pattern for loch or rain-fed river,
a thinly dressed version minus the tippets
tail will often give more modern chironomid
impressions a run for their money.

Hook: *Size 8-12*
Thread: *Black*
Tail: *Golden-pheasant tippets*
Body: *Black floss tied thinly*
Rib: *Fine oval silver tinsel*
Hackle: *Black cock*

Cove Pheasant Tail Nymph

Originally designed to imitate a large brown buzzer, it is a reliable point fly for prospecting the bottom when bank-fishing. Fish it on as long a leader as you can manage with buzzer pupae occupying the dropper positions. The retrieve should be as slow as your patience will allow. The longshank version is a much underestimated pattern to use when trout are feeding on newly hatched fry.

Hook: *Size 8-14 standard and longshank hooks*
Thread: *Black*
Body: *Cock pheasant tail fibres*
Rib: *Seven turns of fine copper wire*
Thorax: *A small round ball of rabbit underfur*
Thorax cover: *Pheasant tail fibres*

Cove's Orange Nymph

This nymph excels on sunny days when rainbows are feeding on daphnia and, curiously enough, when floating snails are high on the menu.

Hook: *Size 10-12 longshank*
Thread: *Brown*
Body: *Orange seal's fur*
Rib: *Flat gold tinsel*
Thorax: *As body*
Thorax cover: *Pheasant tail fibres*

Doobry

This Orcadian pattern is an excellent bob fly
when seeking either brown trout or
rainbows. At its best when fished in coloured
water on a bright day or in clear water
on a dullish day.

Hook: *Size 8-12*
Thread: *Black*
Tag: *Fluorescent-red wool*
Body: *Flat gold tinsel*
Body hackle: *Black cock ribbed with gold wire*
Head hackle: *Hot-orange over-wound*
with longish black hen

Jack Ketch

Definitely one for those who need to fish slow
and deep but who spurn the use of lures.

Hook: *Size 10*
Thread: *Black*
Body: *Silver tip then a dubbed blend of claret, red and
blue seal's fur wound over a lead-foil underbody*
Hackle: *Long black hen*

Invicta

A thinly dressed Invicta is a 'must' fly during a hatch of any small brown sedges. As a high-summer dusk fades into darkness, dunk a thickly hackled version in floatant and fish it singly as a wake fly. Use strong nylon!

Hook: *Size 8-14*
Thread: *Brown or yellow*
Tail: *Golden-pheasant crest*
Body: *Yellow-amber seal's fur or substitute*
Rib: *Oval gold*
Hackle: *Ginger cock palmered down the body*
Wing: *Hen pheasant*
Hackle: *Jay fibres*

Persuader

All of John Goddard's flies are great takers of trout, and none is better than this bright little pattern, which has earned the reputation of being highly effective when fished at any depth and at any speed.

Hook: *Size 8-12*
Thread: *Orange*
Body: *White ostrich herl*
Rib: *Silver tinsel*
Thorax: *Hot-orange seal's fur*
Thorax cover: *Dark-brown pheasant tail fibres*

Poodle

This highly mobile lure is best cast out and almost left to its own devices. The most effective retrieve is one that just keeps pace with the fly as it drifts around on the wind. For such a slowly fished lure, the takes are surprisingly solid.

Hook: *Size 6-10 longshank*
Thread: *Black*
Tail: *Black marabou*
Body: *Black chenille*
Wing: *Four black marabou tufts tied in at intervals along the body to form a crest*

Cased Caddis

Trundling around on the bottom in its little house of sticks and stones, the sedge larva is anything but safe from the attentions of the trout, which eat the juicy grubs, stones and all. Remember the pace of the natural when you retrieve.

Hook: *Size 10-12 longshank*
Thread: *Black*
Underbody: *Fine lead wire*
Body: *Dubbed hare's fur*
Thorax: *White swan herl*
Hackle: *Short black hen*

Connemara Black Bumble

This Irish fly revels in a day of rolling waves and dark skies. Fish it on the top dropper to scurry across the surface.

Hook: *Size 10-14*
Thread: *Black*
Tail: *Golden-pheasant topping*
Body: *Black seal's fur*
Body hackle: *Black cock*
Rib: *Fine oval silver*
Head hackle: *Partridge dyed blue or jay*

Connemara Black

Originally tied as a fly for Irish sea-trout, it is a first-choice top dropper fly on a loch-style leader whenever small black flies are hatching. A jumbo version tied on a fine-wire salmon iron or a lightweight tube is a dapping fly *par excellence*.

Hook: *Size 6-12*
Thread: *Black*
Tail: *Golden-pheasant topping*
Body: *Black seal's fur or substitute*
Rib: *Oval silver tinsel*
Wing: *Bronze mallard*
Hackle: *Black cock or hen with blue jay over*

Mallard and Claret

A reliable fly for loch-style fishing, particularly on a soft, grey day when dark chironomids or sedges are hatching. It can be nothing short of lethal on a stillwater when inched along close to the surface as dusk gives way to darkness.

Hook: *Size 10-14*
Thread: *Black*
Tail: *Golden-pheasant tippets*
Body: *Dark claret seal's fur*
Rib: *Oval silver tinsel*
Wing: *Bronze mallard*
Hackle: *Black or brown hen at the throat*

Montana Nymph

This stillwater angler's jack-of-all-trades
does well in all manner of conditions. It
performs particularly well when presented on
a floating line, long leader and retrieved
slowly.

Hook: *Size 8-10 longshank*
Thread: *Black*
Tail: *Black cock hackle fibres*
Body: *Black chenille*
Thorax: *Yellow or lime-green chenille*
Thorax cover: *Strand of black chenille*
Hackle: *Black cock hackle palmered*
through thorax

Mosely Mayfly

A great fly for both rivers and stillwaters when trout are feeding on newly hatched duns.

Hook: *Size 8-10*
Thread: *Brown*
Rib: *Fine oval gold tinsel*
Tail: *Pheasant tail fibres*
Body: *Equal parts hare's ear and yellow seal's fur*
Hackle: *Tied in a fan-shape on top of the hook. Medium-olive and blue dun cock hackles with a lemon-yellow cock hackle wound through them*

Shredge

Being a passable interpretation of both shrimps and sedges in various stages, a weighted version of this useful hybrid is well worth trying when nothing stirs.

Hook: Size 10-12
Thread: Brown
Body: Mixture of 70 per cent cinnamon, and 30 per cent yellow seal's fur
Rib: Gold wire
Wing: Grey mallard
Hackle: Pale ginger

Teal and Black

A reliable point fly when fishing loch-style in early season. Use a size 8 when fishing for sea-trout at night.

Hook: *Size 8-14*
Thread: *Black*
Tail: *Golden-pheasant tippets*
Body: *Black seal's fur*
Rib: *Fine oval silver*
Wing: *Strongly barred teal*
Hackle: *Black hen or cock*

Viva

Useful the season through, it is effective
when fished at all levels but especially when
retrieved slow and deep to early-season
trout. An effective loch-style variation is
dressed on small doubles and sports
jungle-cock cheeks.

Hook: *Size 8-10 standard and longshank*
Thread: *Black*
Tail: *Fluorescent-green floss*
Body: *Black chenille*
Rib: *Flat or oval silver*
Wing: *Black marabou with a few
strands of Twinkle*

Index

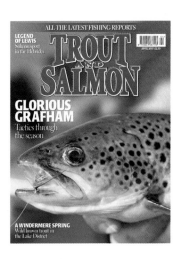